SCHIRMER'S LIBRARY
OF MUSICAL CLASSICS

Vol. 922

GIUSEPPE TARTINI

The Art of Bowing

For the Violin

Fifty Variations on a Gavotte

By Corelli

Edited and Revised by

LEOPOLD LICHTENBERG

G. SCHIRMER, *Inc.*

DISTRIBUTED BY

HAL•LEONARD®
CORPORATION

7777 W. BLUEMOUND RD. P.O. BOX 13819 MILWAUKEE, WI 53213

The Art of Bowing
(L'art de l'archet)

⊓ Down-Bow
V Up-Bow
W. B. Whole Bow
H. B. Half-Bow
Pt Point
Nt Nut
— Sustain
' Martelé
. Spiccato

VIOLIN

GIUSEPPE TARTINI
Edited and revised by
Leopold Lichtenberg

★ The very moderate tempo remains the same, on the whole, throughout the work. The few slight modifications in tempo in the more sustained variations are indicated by the words "tranquillo", "tranquillamente". When played with piano-accompaniment, it is advisable not to observe the repeats.